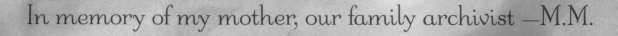

In memory of my mother, our family archivist —M.M.

For my brilliant, magical mother, and for all the women
of the past whose stories have yet to be told —E.S.

Visit us on the Web! rhcbooks.com

Educators and librarians, for a variety of teaching tools,
visit us at RHTeachersLibrarians.com

Library of Congress Cataloging-in-Publication Data
is available upon request.
Library of Congress Control Number: 2017025137
ISBN 978-0-593-80867-2 (trade pbk.)

The illustrations in this book were rendered in
watercolor, gouache, colored pencil, and graphite.
The text of this book is set in Brioso Pro.

MANUFACTURED IN CHINA
10 9 8 7 6 5 4 3 2 1
First Dragonfly Books Edition 2024

In honor of the publication of this book, a contribution has
been made to Graham Windham, the organization Eliza
Hamilton established over two hundred years ago. Today,
Graham Windham is an award-winning organization that
serves nearly 5,000 children and families. In November
2015, Phillipa Soo and Morgan Marcell created the Eliza
Project to give young people served by Graham Windham
the opportunity to use the arts as a means of expression
and to honor Eliza Hamilton's legacy.

Eliza

THE STORY OF
Elizabeth Schuyler Hamilton

WORDS BY

Margaret McNamara

ARTWORK BY

Esmé Shapiro

WITH AN AFTERWORD BY PHILLIPA SOO

Dragonfly Books —✦— New York

July 4, 1854, Washington

My dearly beloved Elizabeth, for I hope that is what you will be called, if you are born a girl,

My daughter, who is your grandmama, has asked me to devote this day to writing a letter to you, about my very long and fortunate life. I am not much given to letter-writing nowadays, nor was I ever inclined to write about myself, yet you may perhaps find much to interest you herein.

Alexander Hamilton

Dolley Madison

Benjamin Franklin

To look at me today, a tiny dot of a woman, you would not know that I once was married to a brilliant man whose name is writ large in history. Nor would you guess that Mr. Benjamin Franklin taught me to play backgammon, or that General Washington and his wife, Martha, were good friends to me.

Together with Mrs. Dolley Madison, the wife of our fourth president, I raised

George Washington

Martha Washington

Franklin Pierce

funds for the Washington Monument, which will one day rise in this city. Indeed, I have met and conversed with all fourteen presidents, among them the odious Mr. John Adams, the despicable Mr. Andrew Jackson, and even the young Mr. Franklin Pierce, who holds the office today.

The legacies of some presidents, my dear, are greater than those of others.

My story began on a hot August day in 1757. My parents, of old Dutch stock, were Philip Schuyler and Catherine van Rensselaer Schuyler and were most prominent in the province of New York. I was given the name Elizabeth, though my family called me sometimes Betsey, and sometimes Eliza, and sometimes Bess, but never Lizzy. Before my birth came that of my sister Angelica, and not long after I was born my mother was delivered of another girl, our dear sister Margarita, called Peggy. My beloved mamma gave birth to fifteen children over the course of her long years, yet fully seven of my brothers and sisters did not survive infancy. It pained my heart, as a child, to think of them. It pains me now.

When I was eight years old, we moved to a grand and formal house, Albany's finest, which my father built at great expense, although to me it was simply home. It sat high on a hill over the Hudson River and could be seen by friend and foe for miles around. Acres of gardens and farms surrounded it, and beyond that, woods and valleys. Our estate was called the Pastures, and I loved the place dearly.

When we were not at our lessons, or at prayer, or sewing or knitting or practicing our instruments, we were free to roam the forest and valleys, the rocks and waterfalls all around us.

That was what I liked to do best—how I laughed when girls from the city came to visit and dared not climb or run for fear of falling!

From Mamma we learned to be good housekeepers, yet even then I was aware that the most difficult tasks in the household were taken up by Silvia and her sons Tom and Hanover—those are the names I remember. And Prince, of course, who was my father's longest-serving help and support. As I grew older, I came to realize it is a great sin, then and now, to hold souls as property, with no freedom, no pay, and no surnames of their own.

When my father died, my brothers, sisters, and I freed them all. And in my later life, I supported my husband as he helped found a school for the children of those who were formerly enslaved.

It seems the day is coming when our country will not permit any human person to be enslaved. I pray nightly I will see that happen in my lifetime.

I have spent too much of this letter on my own history, when the history of the nation was being lived at that moment, too!

When I was born, these United States did not exist. I could count the colonies without reaching twenty. Our government, now situated here in the very city where I write, was far away, in England, and we were ruled by a king.

You, beloved child, will be born in a vast nation whose territories stretch from ocean to ocean. You will grow up with railways that crisscross the continent, and steamships that will travel to lands whose names are unknown to me. You will come of age in a strong and stable country esteemed throughout the world. That is in part because of my adored husband, your great-grandfather Alexander Hamilton.

Of Alexander Hamilton much is known and much more will be written. I have myself spent the better part of fifty years tending his legacy. It is not too much to boast that my Alexander's words swayed the nation to accept our Constitution.

He advised General Washington in war and in peace, and was appointed the first secretary of the Treasury, a tribute to the foresight of his ideas. Without him, this country we live in would be a very different place.

Alexander endured much as a child, abandoned by family and cast out of his island home at fourteen years of age. I, who had every comfort when young, longed to bestow on him the warmth of hearth and home he never knew as a boy. Our courtship took place at the home of my aunt, who lived, at the time, near General Washington's headquarters in the province of New Jersey, and we were married shortly thereafter. Despite the uncertainty of war, those were happy days indeed!

In society, I introduced Alexander to the ladies and gentlemen whose families had first settled America, and smoothed his course as he rose in stature and renown.

In matters of politics, I was his sounding board, and his sometime scribe. When Alexander's hand ached from writing letters teeming with ideas for our new government, I took over his pen so he could rest.

I was his proud wife for nearly twenty-four years, and tended to his needs as he
dedicated himself to his country. Together we raised our eight devoted children,
and took in others who had none to care for them.

Together, too, we weathered the scandal that beset us. And together we mourned our firstborn, Philip, who was killed as a young man, and our cherished daughter, Angelica, who suffered greatly after her brother's death and never recovered. There is not a day that goes by when I do not think of them.

We found solace in the green and verdant countryside of Harlem, just nine short miles outside New York City. Alexander purchased thirty-two acres of land there, and we built a home of our own, which Alexander called the Grange. He drew up careful plans for the garden, and saw to it that thirteen young sweet gum trees were planted on the grounds, in honor of the first thirteen colonies of our young nation. I wonder if those trees yet grow and provide shade.

Then in that most dreadful year of 1804, too soon, I found myself holding Alexander in my arms as he breathed his last, after the duel that took his life. He was just forty-seven years old.

From that time on I have worn, in a velvet pouch about
my neck, a poem composed in my honor by my husband,
nor will it be removed till my dying day.

I did not remarry. Instead, I turned my attention to my family, and Alexander's legacy, and to the pressing needs all around me. Whenever I had a little property I could part with, or extra money to give away, I instructed that the funds be put aside for needy children.

By the grace of God, I was able to donate land and property to build a school not far from the Grange. We called it the Hamilton Free School, in my husband's honor. I did not have to live in splendor when so many around me were wanting.

There was no institution at that time that would take in orphans and give them refuge from the dangerous streets of New York City. Working with devoted ladies from my church, through much persistence and, perhaps, some stubbornness, I raised the necessary funds to establish the Orphan Asylum Society of the City of New York. Many people scoffed at the idea of women attempting such an undertaking, but we were not daunted.

The orphanage opened its doors in the year 1806. It was the first of its kind in the state of New York. We insisted that the director of the institution be faithful, tender, and unremitting in the care of the orphans. I would not stand for unkindness.

By 1837, our orphanage had grown too large for its cramped quarters in Greenwich Village. We erected a modern structure three miles north, in Bloomingdale Village, which housed more than two hundred children.

I am told that those in need still knock on the doors of our orphanage. With God's help, may it outlive us all.

In my long life, I have witnessed much more than I can tell in this writing (although, to be sure, it feels as if the years flew by). I shall add only that I hope to live my remaining days watching my grandchildren and great-grandchildren grow, taking walks and tending my garden, and working ever to keep the flame of history, and especially of my beloved Alexander, alive.

The daylight has dimmed, and truth be told, writing fatigues me. I end this letter, dear child, in all love and tenderness. May God bless you and keep you. My prayer for you is that you live as full a life as I have been granted to live, and that you dedicate yourself to this great country, so that it may truly provide the promise of life and liberty for all.

I am, my dear child, yours ever affectionately,

Elizt Hamilton

Afterword

When I was first asked to portray Eliza Schuyler Hamilton in *Hamilton: An American Musical,* I had no knowledge of who this woman was. Researching the role gave me the chance to learn about her incredible story beyond being the wife of Alexander Hamilton. She was one of America's first female activists and philanthropists, and knowing that helped me to shape who she became onstage.

© Joan Marcus

What amazed me most was Eliza's strength of spirit. She overcame the tragic loss of her husband and lived to the age of ninety-seven, which to me feels like no coincidence. She knew that there was work to be done in her lifetime. While striving to uphold her husband's legacy, she created her own. Eliza achieved much in her long life, from raising funds for the Washington Monument to speaking out against slavery to her greatest accomplishment—establishing the first private orphanage in New York City.

Shortly after I was cast in *Hamilton,* I discovered that the orphanage still exists today, and I decided to pay it a visit. My experience that day at what is now called Graham Windham, a social service organization that helps families and children in the New York area, was more valuable than any single piece of information about Eliza. I was a witness to her life's work. I had an opportunity not only to learn about her legacy, but also to become a part of it. I learned that the energy and love we put into our life's work can carry on without us, as hers did. And I learned that it's possible for our hopes and dreams to manifest themselves far after we leave this world—they are the seeds of our future.

I am so glad that people will finally hear more of Eliza's story in this picture book and that they too can be inspired by her strength, her hard work, and her endless capacity for love. She was truly the "best of wives and best of women."

Phillipa Soo

My dear Reader,

Elizabeth Schuyler Hamilton wrote many, many letters in her lifetime. Very few of them survive. After walking through the rooms of Eliza's family home in Albany, biking past a brownstone where she lived in New York's East Village, sitting under the trees at her house in Harlem, and holding one of her letters in my hand at the New-York Historical Society, I was inspired to write this book in Eliza's voice. Here are some notes to help fill out the details of Eliza's life and legacy.

Elizabeth Schuyler Hamilton (August 9, 1757–November 9, 1854) was married to the American statesman Alexander Hamilton (January 11, 1755 or 1757–July 12, 1804) and was the earliest archivist of his letters; she was also the cofounder of the Orphan Asylum Society of the City of New York. Witness to nearly one hundred years of the history of the United States, Eliza was devoted to her family, to her husband's memory, and to taking care of those less fortunate than herself.

pp. 2–37 The imaginary letter that is the text of this book is set in the last year of Eliza's life. At that time, her grandson Alexander and his wife were expecting a baby. That baby, a girl, was born on January 19, 1855, and was named Maria Elizabeth Hamilton.

pp. 4–5 Eliza was considered to be like royalty by Americans in the early days of the republic and was acquainted with all fourteen presidents who served during her lifetime. Her antipathy for John Adams is well known, and from studying Eliza's letters and life's work, I conjectured that she considered Andrew Jackson a very bad president: a slave-owner who defied rulings made by the United States courts, he ordered the slaughter of thousands of people of the Creek, Cherokee, and other nations. Both Eliza and Dolley Madison attended the ground-breaking ceremony for the Washington Monument on July 4, 1848. (Congressman Abraham Lincoln was also in attendance.) Eliza did not live to see the completion of the monument, however. Construction was halted in the years before and during the Civil War, and the structure was completed in 1884.

pp. 6–9 Eliza's family wealth came largely from wheat, flax, and lumber harvested on land owned by the Schuylers in the Saratoga region of what is now New York State. The Dutch settlers—among them Eliza's ancestors—were responsible for taking land from the Haudenosaunee people, who occupied and settled the region for thousands of years before the arrival of the Europeans. Eliza's father, in particular, became wealthy through corrupt political and economic deals that allowed him to acquire land cheaply from the Haudenosaunee and then to sell it at much higher prices.

pp. 10–11 Eliza grew up roaming the rocky, forested, mountainous terrain of the Adirondacks. When she was in her teens, her family was visited by the Lynches of South Carolina. Eliza and the younger Lynches took a trip to the waterfalls near the Pastures, where Eliza surprised the southern ladies with her fearlessness.

pp. 12–13 There are no portraits of the people who were enslaved by the Schuyler family, so no one can be sure what they looked like. With the exception of a man called Prince, the personal details of those people are not well documented: their names have come to light only recently, thanks to the work of researchers at the Pastures. (The Pastures is now called the Schuyler Mansion State Historic Site and is open to the public.) Based on Eliza's actions throughout her life, particularly her support of the African Free School, funded in part by donations from her and her husband, I imagined that in her old age she continued to condemn the institution of slavery.

pp. 14–15 In Eliza's lifetime, the United States grew from a small cluster of provinces to a single nation that stretched three thousand miles, from the Atlantic to the Pacific. The population of the country grew from fewer than three million people to over twenty-three million. By 1869, the Transcontinental Railroad connected the East Coast to the West Coast. Large cities grew up. People communicated via a sophisticated postal system and lightning-quick telegraphs. The United States of America was a large and rich country, and able to stand on its own. Many historians believe America owed much of its success to Alexander Hamilton.

pp. 16–19 Alexander Hamilton, soldier, statesman, first secretary of the Treasury, was born on the Caribbean island of Nevis on January 11, 1755 (or 1757; historians disagree on the date). He was abandoned by his father at a young age, and, with his brother, James, mostly had to fend for himself. As a teenager, after writing a vivid account of a hurricane that ravaged the Caribbean in 1772, he made the passage to America. He was admitted to King's College, quickly earned his bachelor's degree, and was known for his speeches in fierce opposition to British rule of the Colonies.

During the American Revolution, Hamilton distinguished himself on the battlefields and as an aide to George Washington,

and became Washington's personal secretary. After his marriage to Eliza in 1780 and the surrender of the British at Yorktown in 1781, he practiced law in New York and served in the Continental Congress. He founded the Bank of New York in 1784.

In 1787, Hamilton was one of the writers of a series of essays defending the United States Constitution, known as the Federalist Papers. He was named secretary of the Treasury when George Washington was elected president in 1789. Despite some rocky periods, he and Washington remained close friends throughout their political lives. Hamilton's influence on American political and financial policy continues to the present day.

pp. 18–20 In the eighteenth century, men and women often powdered their hair or wore powdered wigs to make themselves look more distinguished, especially on formal occasions.

pp. 22–23 Alexander and Elizabeth had eight children. The illustration of Eliza, Alexander, and their children is set at their home in New York City in 1792. Depicted in the painting from left to right are Alexander Junior, six years old; Alexander Hamilton; Angelica, eight years old; Fanny Antill, the Hamiltons' adopted daughter, six years old; Philip, ten years old; James, four years old; and baby John, in his mother's arms.

p. 24 In the summer of 1797, Alexander admitted that he had had an affair with another woman, and that the woman's husband had blackmailed him. A few years later, in 1801, Eliza lost her beloved sister Peggy, and the Hamiltons' son Philip died in a duel defending his father's reputation. A duel was a way to resolve an argument in which two men shot at each other; the practice was largely abandoned by the mid-nineteenth century. Soon after Philip's death, the Hamiltons' daughter Angelica suffered a mental breakdown. It was a tragic time for Eliza.

p. 25 Alexander oversaw every aspect of the construction of the Grange, the Hamiltons' country estate in Harlem. The house sat on some thirty-two acres and had a view of rolling hills and the East River. Named in honor of the estate of Alexander's ancestors in Scotland, it was the first house Alexander and Eliza owned themselves. The thirteen trees Alexander planted are no longer growing on the grounds, but the house and garden are now a National Historic site.

p. 26 On July 12, 1804, in an echo of what happened to his son, Alexander himself died after being mortally wounded by his political opponent Aaron Burr in a duel. The nation was shocked to lose a leading light of American politics.

p. 27 The small velvet pouch Eliza wore around her neck after Alexander's death held a sonnet written to her by Alexander soon after they met. It includes the lines *Before no mortal ever knew / A love like mine so tender, true.* . . . She patched and repaired the pouch many times, and wore it until the day she died.

Almost immediately after Alexander died, Eliza started to collect his letters, essays, and other writings. She knew they would be an important part of American history. Eliza also worked with writers to produce the first biography of Alexander Hamilton. These projects occupied her throughout the rest of her life.

pp. 28–29 Alexander left Eliza with a lot of debts to pay. It was only Eliza's own careful management of the household finances that kept her family afloat. Still, she found time and money to give to others. In the early nineteenth century there was no public school system. The Hamilton Free School provided education for local children whose parents could not afford to pay for schooling.

pp. 30–33 By 1806, Eliza—working with two fellow parishioners of Trinity Church, Isabella Graham and Johanna Bethune—had founded the Orphan Asylum Society of the City of New York (*asylum* means "a place of refuge"). It was the first orphanage in New York City and in the state of New York. When the orphanage opened its doors, it had to turn away all but sixteen of the two hundred children who needed help. Eliza quickly got to work to raise more money to expand the asylum. But she did more than just raise money for the orphanage: she was the "first directress" (or president) of the organization for twenty-seven years and served on the board of trustees for forty-two years. The orphanage soon outgrew its first homes and moved to a much larger building on what is now New York's Upper West Side.

pp. 34–37 When Eliza was older and her children were grown, she moved to Washington, D.C., to live with her youngest daughter, Eliza, and her family. She was never idle. Along with Dolley Madison, Eliza raised money for the Washington Monument, and attended its ground-breaking in 1848. (The future President Lincoln was there, too.) When she was ninety-two, Eliza attended a celebratory service marking the fortieth anniversary of the orphanage she had helped build. She tried to enter quietly, but the entire congregation stood and applauded when they recognized her.

Eliza died peacefully on November 9, 1854. Thanks to her efforts, her husband's legacy lives on, and the institution she founded still opens its doors to needy families.

Affectionately,
M. McNamara

SELECTED BIBLIOGRAPHY

Board of the Orphan Asylum of the City of New York. *Constitution, and By-Laws, of the Orphan Asylum, of the City of New-York*, Samuel Wood. New-York: 1815.

Boylan, Anne M. *The Origins of Women's Activism: New York and Boston 1797–1840*. Chapel Hill: University of North Carolina Press, 2002.

Chernow, Ron. *Alexander Hamilton*. New York: Penguin, 2005.

Desmond, Alice Curtis. *Alexander Hamilton's Wife: A Romance of the Hudson*. New York: Dodd, Mead and Company, 1954.

Hamilton, Alexander, Elizabeth Hamilton, Angelica Hamilton, et al. Letters. Founders Online. founders.archives.gov/about/Hamilton.

Hamilton, Elizabeth Schuyler. Letters. New-York Historical Society.

Hauptman, Laurence M. *Conspiracy of Interests: Iroquois Dispossession and the Rise of New York State*. Syracuse, NY: Syracuse University Press, 2001.

Miranda, Lin-Manuel. *Hamilton: The Revolution*. New York: Grand Central Publishing, 2016.

Tilghman, Tench. *Memoir of Lieut. Col. Tench Tilghman, Secretary and Aid to Washington*. Albany, NY: J. Munsell, 1876.

WEBSITES OF INTEREST

Founders Online: founders.archives.gov

Graham Windham: graham-windham.org

Hamilton Grange National Memorial: nps.gov/hagr/index.htm

New-York Historical Society: nyhistory.org

Schuyler Mansion State Historic Site: parks.ny.gov/historic-sites/33/details.aspx

Trinity Church Wall Street: trinitywallstreet.org

CHRONOLOGY

1755: September. Philip Schuyler and Catherine van Rensselaer marry in Albany, New York.

1755: Alexander Hamilton is born on the island of Nevis in the Caribbean. (Some accounts report this date as 1757.)

1757: August 9. Eliza is born in Albany, New York.

1765: The Schuyler family takes up residence at the Pastures.

1773: Alexander Hamilton arrives in New York.

1776: The Declaration of Independence is sent to King George III.

1780: February. Eliza meets Alexander Hamilton while staying at the home of her father's sister, Gertrude Schuyler Cochran, in Morristown, New Jersey.

1780: December 14. Elizabeth Schuyler and Alexander Hamilton are married at the Pastures.

1781: British General Cornwallis surrenders at Yorktown, Virginia.

1787: The African Free School opens its doors.

1797: Hamilton publishes the Reynolds Pamphlet, admitting to an extra-marital affair with Maria Reynolds.

1801: Philip Hamilton is killed by George Eacker in a duel.

1802: Eliza and Alexander complete work on the Grange, their estate in Harlem, New York.

1803: Catherine Schuyler, Eliza's mother, dies in Albany.

1804: Alexander Hamilton is killed in a duel with Aaron Burr. Philip Schuyler, Eliza's father, dies in Albany.

1807: The Orphan Asylum Society of New York opens its doors.

1808: The Orphan Asylum moves to larger quarters in Greenwich Village.

1818: The Hamilton Free School opens in what is now Washington Heights, New York.

1820: The Orphan Asylum outgrows its second home and moves to what is now the Upper West Side of Manhattan.

1831: Eliza commissions a biography of Hamilton, to be written by Francis Baylies. Baylies does not complete the book. Instead, the biography is completed by James Hamilton after Eliza's death.

1837: Eliza is successful in petitioning the United States government to pay her the widow's pension she was owed after Hamilton's death.

1840: With her daughter Elizabeth, Eliza makes the thousand-mile journey from Washington, D.C., to Hamilton's Diggings in the Northwest Territory (now Wisconsin) to visit her son William.

1846: Eliza attends the fortieth anniversary of the founding of the Orphan Asylum.

1854: November 9. Elizabeth dies at her daughter's home in Washington, D.C.

2018 and beyond: The Orphan Asylum Society of New York, now called Graham Windham, continues to help needy children and their families.

ACKNOWLEDGMENTS

The author and artist wish to acknowledge the invaluable aid in the research of this book provided by Tammy Kiter, Manuscript Reference Librarian, the New-York Historical Society; Heidi Hill, Site Manager, and Danielle Funicello and Ian Mumpton, Historical Interpreters, Schuyler Mansion Historic Site, for their insight into Eliza's world; the staff of Hamilton Grange National Memorial; Phyllis Barr, Graham Windham Historian Archivist; Professor Jane Mt. Pleasant, Cornell University; and the staff of the New York Society Library. Special thanks to the artist's research assistant, Anna Kaufman, and to Anne Schwartz, Rachael Cole, William Vogan, and most ardently, Lee Wade, who gave us the gift of Eliza.